Rodolphe
KREUTZER

FORTY-TWO STUDIES
OR CAPRICES

FOR VIOLIN

K 03594

Kalmus

Born at Versailles the 16th of Nov., 1766, of German parentage, **RODOLPHE KREUTZER** enjoyed to the full the advantages of musical lineage and environment. From his father, a violinist in the Royal Band, he received his first lessons in music, and early manifested extraordinary musical talent, with a decided predilection for the violin. Anton Stamitz, a violinist of repute, instructed him in violin-playing for a time; he later learned much from hearing Viotti, and may have received direct instruction from the latter.

At twelve, his playing was distinguished by brilliancy and *verve;* at thirteen, he composed his first violin-concerto, which he himself performed with great applause at one of the *Concerts Spirituels* in Paris. At this time he was often invited to the Trianon, where he sang with taste in the *petits concerts* of the Queen, besides enchanting the select company by his performances on his favorite instrument. In 1782, when but 16, he became first violinist in the royal orchestra, thanks to the good offices of his protectress, Marie Antoinette; taking the position then made vacant by his father's decease. Eight years thereafter, his indomitable perseverance smoothed the way to his appointment as solo violinist at the Théâtre Italien (afterwards the Opéra Comique); his position and influence were now such as to enable him to bring out his first opera, *Jeanne d'Arc à Orléans*, the first in a series of more than 40 dramatic works and ballets produced between 1790 and 1825, in part at the above theatre, in part at the Grand Opera.

During and after the Revolution, Kreutzer seems to have adapted himself with facility to his changing surroundings; there is no noticeable break in his productivity and his general artistic success. He wrote with apparently equal nonchalance the operas designed to delight the unfortunate royal family, those celebrating the events of the bloody social upheaval, and his dramas of the Consulate and the Empire.—Imagine Wagner under like circumstances!—In 1802 he was first violin in the orchestra of the Consul Bonaparte; in 1806, solo violinist of the Emperor Napoleon; in 1815, *maître de chapelle* to Louis XVIII. Kreutzer was, indeed, a musician who lived in and for his art; transient externalities influenced him only in so far as they furnished new material for his facile fancy to work with.

In 1796 he made an extended tour through Italy, Germany, and the Netherlands, on returning from which he was appointed professor of violin at the newly founded Paris Conservatory. Here he entered upon a new phase of professional activity, and soon attracted and developed numerous distinguished pupils. The teachings of Viotti were now bearing fruit; Kreutzer's brilliant and fascinating style won the enthusiastic admiration and confidence of the students, and placed him in the front rank of contemporary virtuosi. He owed this remarkable success to a naturally fine musical instinct, and zeal for art, rather than to strict schooling or study. His execution was characterized by fiery energy, great purity and breadth of tone, nobility of phrasing, and that indescribable individualism of interpretation which is the birthright of genius alone.

In 1801 he advanced to Rode's place as solo violinist at the Grand Opera, of which, in 1816, he was made second, and in 1817 first, *chef d'orchestre.* All this time, Kreutzer was still passionately devoted to composition,—not solely for the lyric stage, but also for his chosen instrument. Works of this latter description are 19 concertos, 15 string-quartets and as many trios, various duos, *symphonies concertantes*, sonatas, airs with variations, etc. ; and with these, the work on which his fame as a composer chiefly rests, namely, the "42 Studies" (often published in an incomplete edition of but 40 numbers). Kreutzer, a leader of that renowned school of violin-playing which originated in Italy, and was further developed in France by Viotti, Baillot, Rode, and himself, gave to posterity, in these "42 Études ou Caprices pour le Violon," a work which still of right occupies a prominent place in every course of violin-training,—which is, in fact, a classic in its province, and indispensable in laying a firm foundation for violin-technique, and as a preparation for the more difficult "24 Caprices" by Rode.

Another work which has served—though in a different way—to embalm his memory, is Beethoven's *Kreutzer Sonata*, dedicated in 1806 to "his friend" Kreutzer. In the dearth of positive information—even Thayer dismisses the subject in a few words—we can only conjecture the extent of the friendship between the two; it is averred that Kreutzer, who visited Vienna in 1798, never even played the sonata, and had but scant sympathy for Beethoven's style.

He was created a Knight of the Legion of Honor in 1824. In the same year he exchanged his post as *chef d'orchestre* for that of general director of the music at the Grand Opera; but held this position only until 1826, then retiring on a pension. In 1825, the breaking of an arm compelled his retirement from the Conservatory and concert stage. Having written a last opera, *Mathilde*, with unwonted care, he confidently applied, in 1827, to the then Director for its production; but his solicitations were in vain. Mortified by this repulse, and a prey to mortal disease, he lingered for some years near the scene of his life-long triumphs. Advised to try the air of Switzerland for the benefit of his health, he proceeded thither in 1831; but it was too late. He expired in Geneva on June the 6th, 1831. It is related that a priest of that town refused him Christian burial, on the ground that he had been connected with the theatre.

Explanation of the Signs.

V Up - bow.   Pt., Point.
⊓ Down-bow.   HB., half-bow.
Iᵃ E-string.   WB., whole bow.
IIᵃ A-string.
IIIᵃ D-string.
IVᵃ G-string.
— hold the finger down.

Forty-two Studies.

R. KREUTZER.

Adagio sostenuto.

This Étude may be practised with the same bowings as the preceding.
Allegro moderato.

3.

The staccato must be practised very slowly to begin with, detaching all notes evenly with a loose wrist, so that the bow does not quit the string. This is a sure way to learn this style of bowing well.

8

This stroke must be executed firmly near the point of the bow, and all the notes must be perfectly e-
ven in point of loudness, this evenness being attained by stronger pressure on the notes taken with up-bow,
as these are naturally more difficult to emphasize than those with down-bow.

Bowing as in the preceding Étude.

Allegro assai.

7.

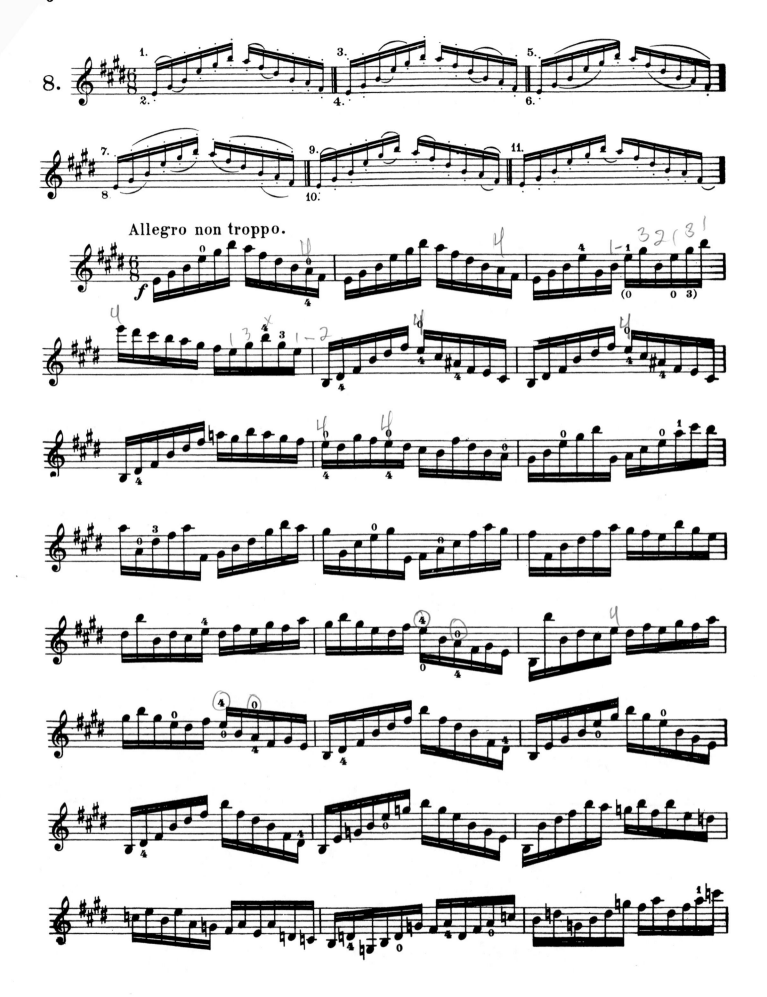

Allegro moderato.

9.

16

Andante.
Shift lightly and rapidly, so that no intermediate tones can be heard.

Moderato.
Keep the fingers down wherever possible.

Moderato. *(Tranquillo.)*

14.

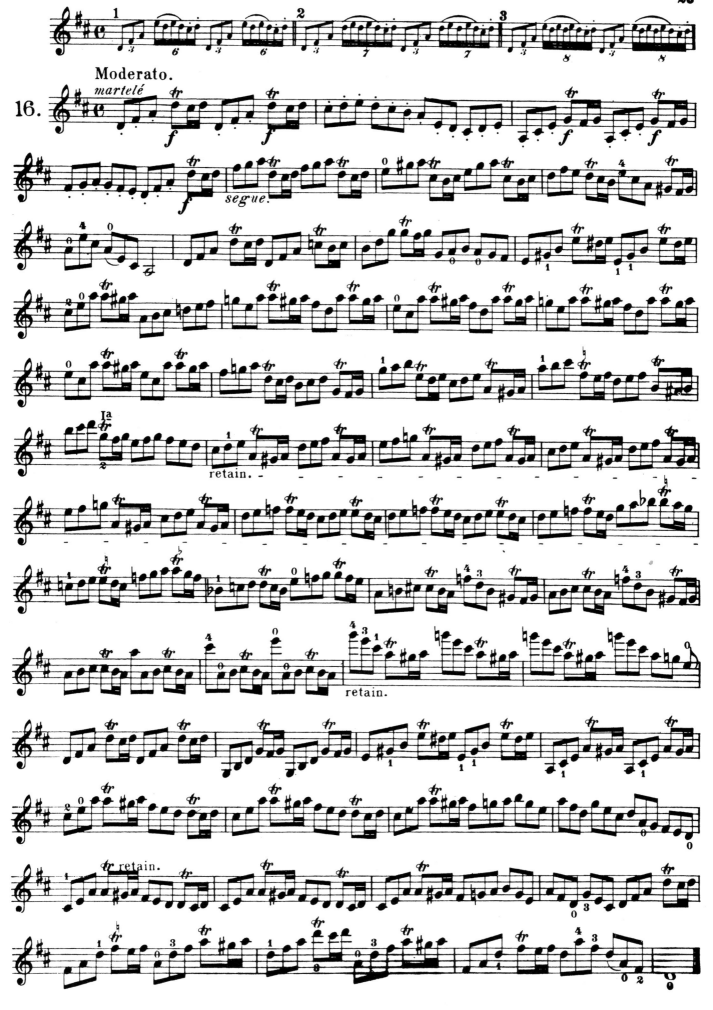

Moderato.

16.

Maestoso.

17.

retain

19.

Moderato.

a) See Étude № 18, Note b.

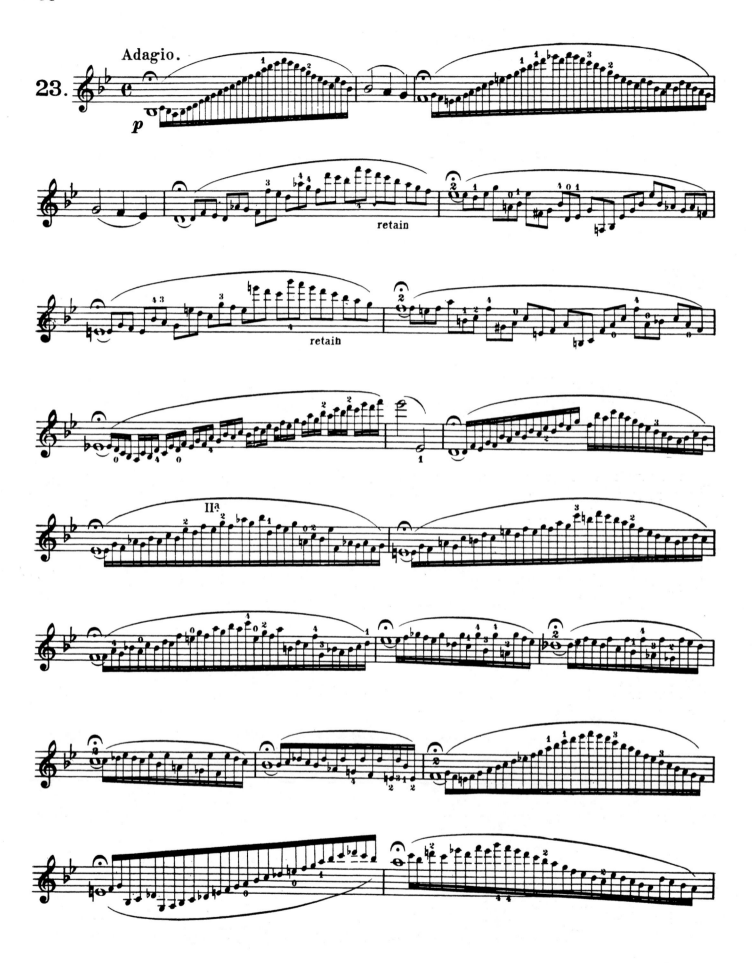

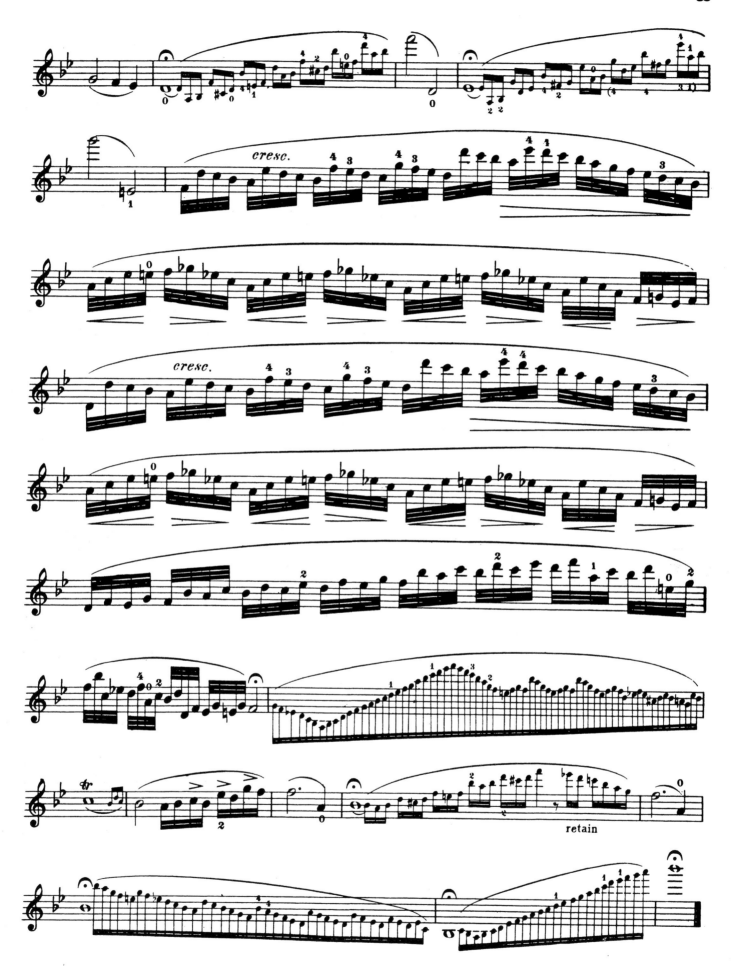

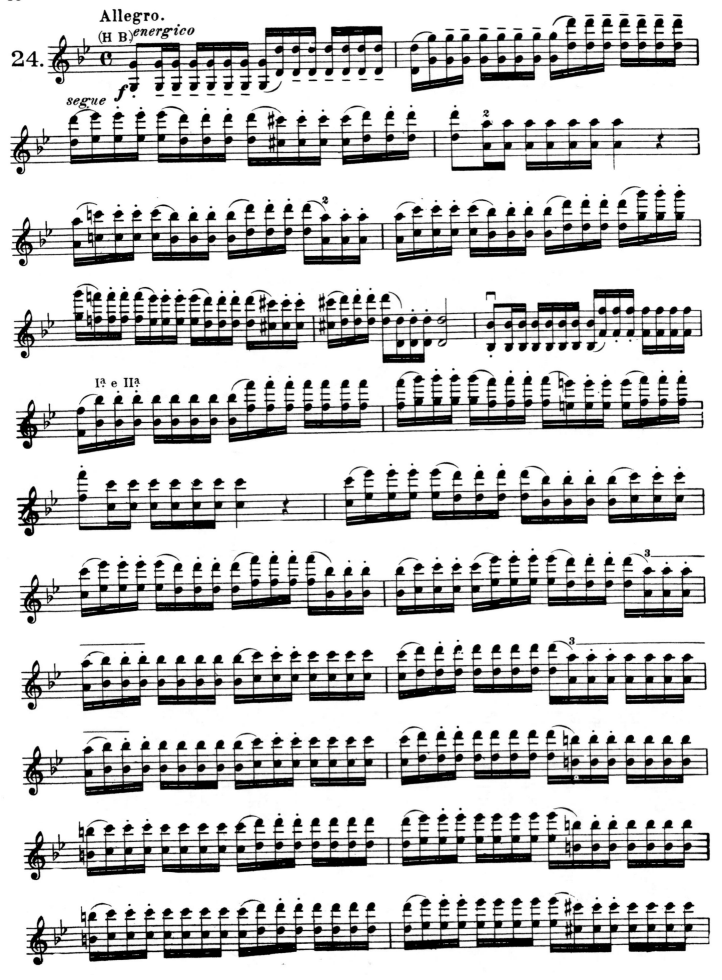

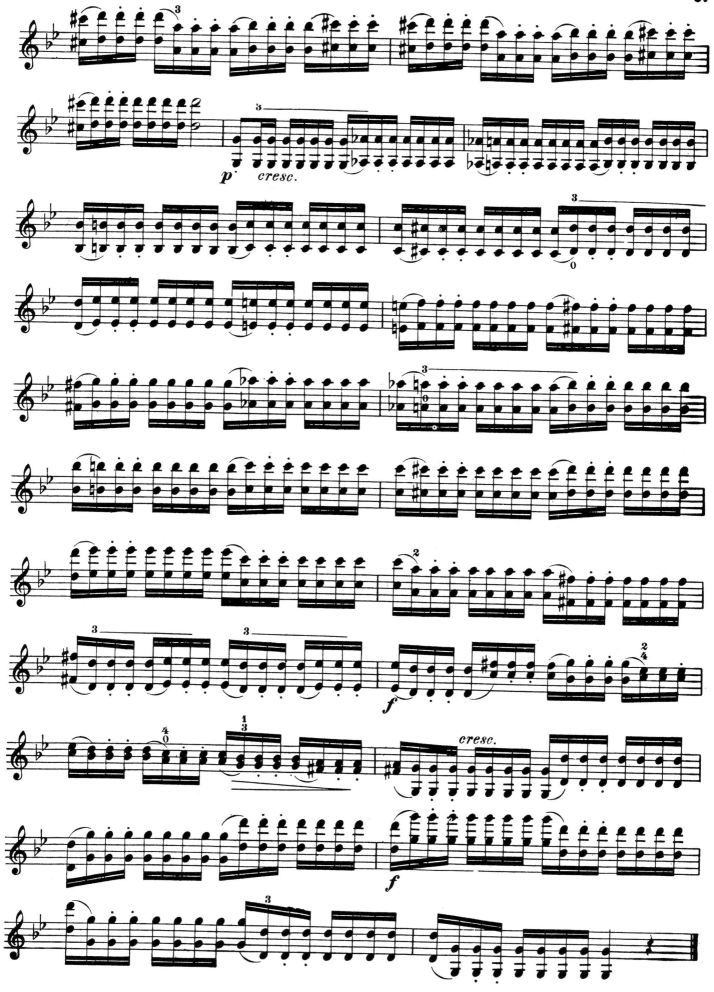

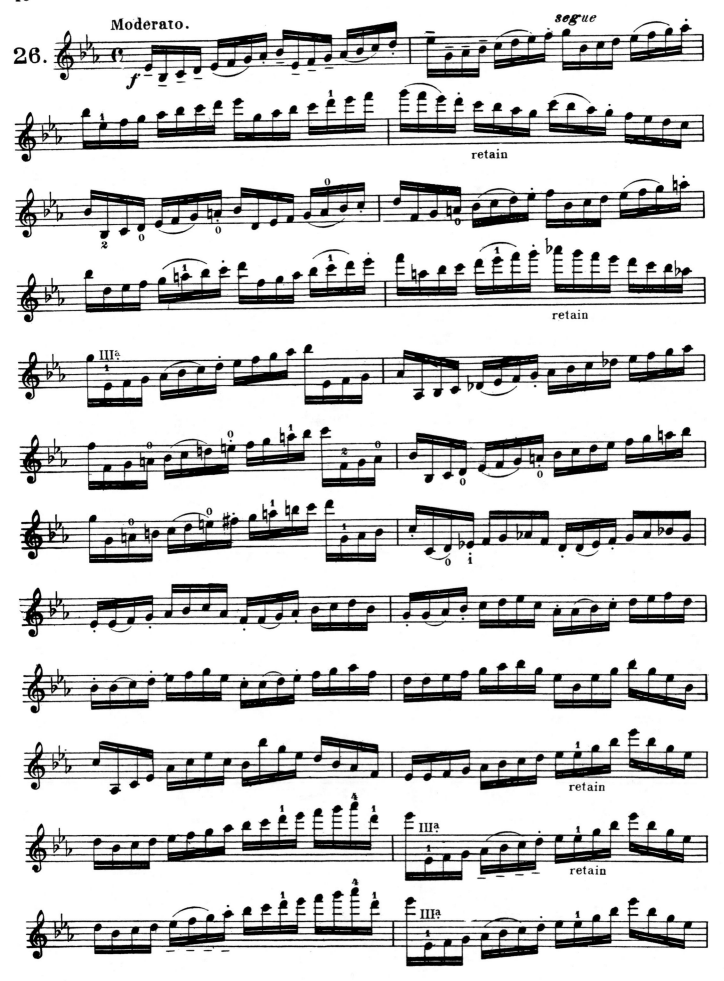

Moderato.

Upper half of bow.

27.

segue

retain

retain

+) Firm staccato at the point.

Moderato. *Tranquilly and very evenly.*

29.

WB. Nut.

50

Allegro.

31.

retain

Practise at first with 2 bows for each measure.

Andante.

32.

34. Moderato.

March.

Allegro maestoso.

35.

58

Allegro Vivace.

37.

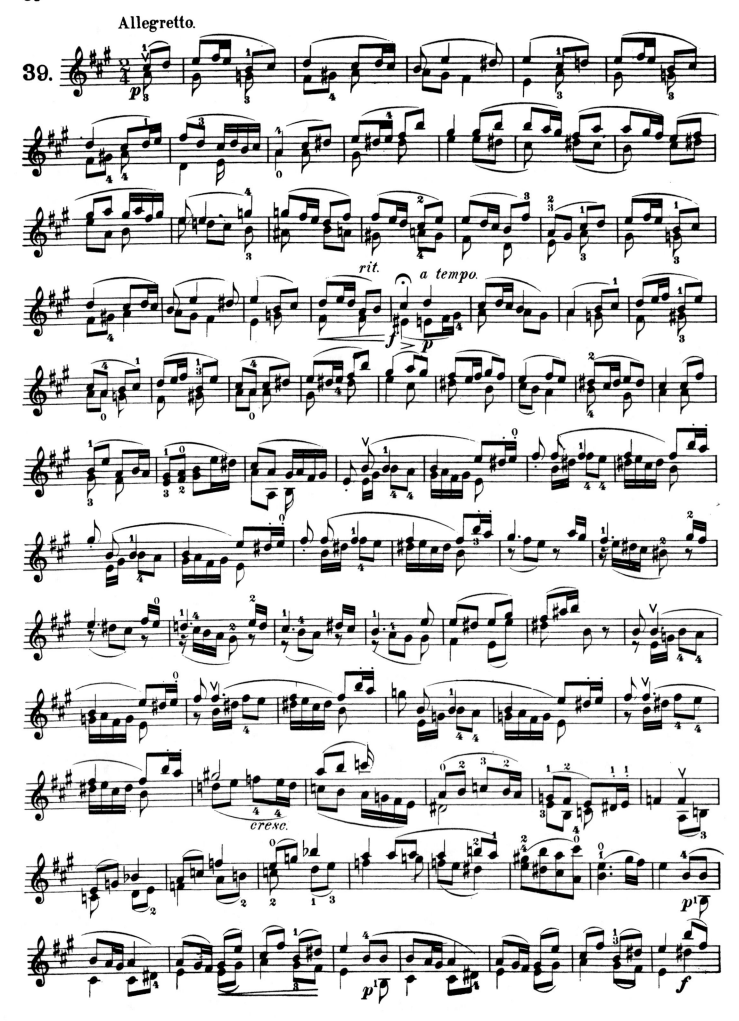

Moderato.
leggiero staccato.

42.